BIRMINGHAM IN THE FIFTIES

VOL 1

Alton & Jo Douglas

Dale End, from High Street, 23rd June 1955. The News Theatre and Albert Street are on the right.

© 1997 Alton and Jo Douglas
ISBN 1 85858 104 4
Published by Brewin Books, Doric House, Church Street, Studley, Warwickshire B80 7LG.
Printed by Warwick Printing Co. Ltd., Theatre Street, Warwick CV34 4DR.
Layout by Alton and Jo Douglas
6th Impression January 2000

Corporation Street with, on the right, Martineau Street in the early stages of demolition, 13th October 1959.
Rackhams is being constructed in the bottom left hand corner.

Front cover: New Street, with the Times building (now Waterstones) on the left, 8th January 1958.
Today, the Rotunda is on this site.

Contents

BREWIN BOOKS

Doric House, Church Street
Studley, Warwickshire B80 7LG

Tel: 01527 854228 Fax: 01527 852746

Vat Registration No. 378 1070 47

Dear Nostalgic,

Are you ready again for more of our time travelling?

Some years ago, on a bus, the man next to me, completely out of the blue, said, "Hasn't this week gone quickly!". I thought, then, what a daft remark it was, almost as if he thought we'd shared all the same experiences. Now, looking back at the 50's, however, it seems as if we could all say, "Didn't that decade go quickly!". So much happened; the Festival of Britain, the Coronation, Warwickshire winning the Championship and Villa the Cup, the ascent of Everest, the trad boom and rock and roll, Teddy boys, Vespas and Lambrettas, bubble-cars, variety and pop stars galore visiting the city and so on.

It was an age of much-loved buildings coming down and soon-to-be-detested monstrosities going up. But it was also an age of hope. What ambitions we all had! I wanted to lead a big band but, in the event, the nearest I got to an eighteen piece orchestra was to front a quartet. These days I have no complaints about the way my life has turned out but I could never have guessed, at the time, what surprises lay ahead. What about you? How did you fare? Did your fluffy clouds turn out to have silver linings?

Anyway, in the 50's, the future lay mysteriously ahead. Let's go back in time to remind ourselves of how we looked and behaved and dreamed our dreams.

Yours, in friendship,

Alton

Rob Pryke (right) leading market trader and councillor, sets off with comedienne, Beryl Reid, in a 1907 Model T Ford, festooned with bananas, to open his "Banana Room" in Curzon Street. Bull Ring, 17th July 1957.

1950

The bad weather brings the traffic to a halt, Corporation Street, January 1950.

Snow Hill, 18th January 1950.

The Alexandra Theatre, Birmingham, is expected to be filled on February 17 for a variety concert organised in aid of "Old Ben" (the Newsvendors' Benevolent and Provident Institution). Artists who will appear include Dennis Noble, the Arden Singers, Dick Lawler, La Mysteree, Harry Engleman and his Players, Ernest Elliott, Joan Butler, Jenson Leng, Philip Cranmer, Beryl Reid, Leslie Welch and Tony Hancock.

EARLY RESULTS TELEVISED

Television played its part in the election for the first time, and viewers were given the early results on a screen in the studio as they were flashed to the crowds in Trafalgar square, writes the radio correspondent.

In Birmingham reception was good and demonstrations were staged by some dealers and manufacturers.

THE calm of the election campaign erupted into noisy, boisterous excitement in Birmingham streets early today. Cheers and counter-cheers met the results flashed on screens or posted on the Town Hall walls.

It was Birmingham's biggest ever poll. Total votes cast were 626,823, equal to about 81.90 per cent. of the electorate of three-quarters of a million, compared with 61 per cent. in 1945.

Enthusiastic crowds greeted Labour's substantial victory of nine seats against the Conservative's four.

The ten Liberals, three Communists, and the one Ind. Pacifist all forfeited their deposits.

Hundreds of people crowded Victoria Square. They became argumentative; split into factions and shouted jibes at each other.

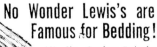

How they voted in BIRMINGHAM

24.2.50

ASTON
*W. L. WYATT (Lab) ... 28,367
C. Doughty (C) 16,826
A. Embrey (Lib) 1,437
W. Keatley (Ind) 338

Majority 12,041
No change

Wyatt (Lab.) 15,031
Normansell (C) 9,264
Lab. majority 5,767

ERDINGTON
*J. SILVERMAN (Lab)... 29,252
J. A. Wright (C) 23,842
J. A. Fitzgerald (Lib) 3,408

Majority 5,410
No change

Silverman (Lab.) 34,786
Wright (C.) 22,457
Lab. majority 12,329

EDGBASTON
*Sir P. BENNETT (C) ... 29,404
J. A. Hobson (Lab) 17,512

Majority 11,892
No change

Bennett (C.) 21,497
Barrow (Lab.) 12,879
Shenfield (L.) 5,832
C. majority 8,618
68 spoilt papers.
Poll 79 p.c.

HALL GREEN
A. JONES (C) 24,444
T. Crehan (Lab) 20,591
G. L. Roy (Lib) 3,703

Majority 3,853
Reorganised constituency

HANDSWORTH
*H. ROBERTS (C) 24,246
C. R. Bence (Lab) 18,774
R. W. Eades (Lib) 4,926

Majority 5,472
No change

Roberts (C.) 15,607
Bence (Lab.) 14,142
Tiptaft (Ind.) 5,112
Mrs. Lewis (L.) 4,945
Mrs. Eden (Comm.) 1,390
C. majority 1,465

KING'S NORTON
Geoffrey LLOYD (C) 27,303
A. F. Bradbeer (Lab) ... 21,715
J. Beesley (Lib) 4,940

Majority 5,593
Blackburn (Lab.) 32,062
Pato (C.) 19,764
White (L.) 6,289
Lab. majority 12,298

LADYWOOD
*V. F YATES (Lab) 25,603
F. Bernett (C.) 16,071

Majority 9,532
No change
Thirty-eight spoilt papers.
Poll 80 p.c.

Yates (Lab.) 13,503
Lloyd (C.) 10,657
Lab majority 2,846

NORTHFIELD
*A. R. BLACKBURN
(Lab) 26,714
T. L. Iremonger (C) 19,974
E. Richards (Lib) 3,280
D. Etheridge (Comm) ... 479

Majority 6,740
Reorganised constituency

PERRY BARR
*C. C. POOLE (Lab) 23,178
Sir Edward Boyle (C) ... 15,172
Mrs. N. Hinks (Lib) 2,581

Majority 8,006
Reorganised constituency
Spoilt papers 16. Total poll 40,947—over 80 p.c.

SMALL HEATH
*F. LONGDEN (Lab) ... 31,985
J. Pagett (C) 15,556
F. G. Smith (Lib) 3,365

Majority 16,429
Reorganised constituency

SPARKBROOK
*P. L. E. SHURMER
(Lab) 24,942
P. Debenham (C) 15,267
J. Crump (Comm) 355

Majority 9,675
No change

Shurmer (Lab.) 14,065
Amery (C.) 8,431
Dutt (Comm.) 1,853
Lab. majority 5,634

STECHFORD
*R. JENKINS (Lab) 33,077
Miss Edith Pitt (C) 20,699
S. W. Haslam (Lib) 2,739

Majority 12,378
Reorganised constituency

YARDLEY
*H. C. USBORNE (Lab)... 22,342
G. Matthews (C) 18,431
A. S. Ritchie (Lib) 2,553
J. Falconer (Comm) 347

Majority 3,911
No change

Perrins (Lab.) 33,855
Salt (C.) 16,514
Middleton (L.) 5,383
Lab majority 17,321

THE sweets ration goes up from 4½oz. to 5oz. a week from tomorrow. The announcement of this temporary increase came from the Ministry of Food yesterday just one hour after the Minister, Mr. Strachey, had been re-elected in Dundee West.

By normal practice the announcement would have been made three days beforehand—on Polling Day—said the Ministry. But Mr Strachey deliberately held up the news so that it could not be interpreted as electioneering.

Allocation of dried eggs for priority consumers ends after today—when shell eggs should be more plentiful.

25.2.50

Bakelite Ltd., Redfern Road, Tyseley, 1950.

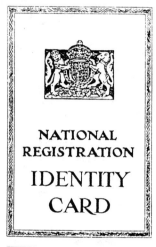

NOTICE   HH 043991

1. Always carry your Identity Card. You may be required to produce it on demand by a Police Officer in uniform or member of H.M. Armed Forces in uniform on duty.

2. You are responsible for this Card, and must not part with it to any other person. You must report at once to the local National Registration Office if it is lost, destroyed, damaged or defaced.

3. If you find a lost Identity Card or have in your possession a Card not belonging to yourself or anyone in your charge you must hand it in at once at a Police Station or National Registration Office.

4. Any breach of these requirements is an offence punishable by a fine or imprisonment or both.

FOR AUTHORISED ENDORSEMENTS ONLY

NATIONAL REGISTRATION IDENTITY CARD

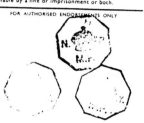

QCBG	158 : 1	SURNAME

CHRISTIAN NAMES (First only in full)

Edmund, C.

CLASS CODE

A.

FULL POSTAL ADDRESS

218 Harborne Lane Birmingham 29 OAA.

HOLDER'S SIGNATURE

CHANGES OF ADDRESS. No entry except by National Registration Officer, to whom removal must be notified.

REMOVED TO (Full Postal Address)

WARD

Re-issued

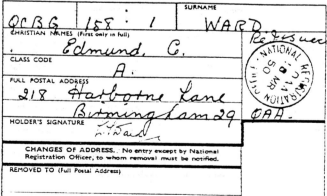

Hay Hall Road, Acocks Green, 1950.

The Circle, Kingstanding, 13th March 1950. The films showing at the Odeon were Barbara Stanwyck in "The File on Thelma Jordon" and John Payne in "Captain China".

Moseley Road, 16th April 1950.

Bull Ring, c 1950.

Malcolm Bottrill, with a model aeroplane made by his dad, in the back garden of their home, Wright Road, Saltley, Summer 1950.

Girls' Brigade Display Team, Watford Road Congregational Church, c 1950.

Comedian, Cyril Fletcher, surrounded by competitors in Lewis's beauty competition, 14th June 1950. The winner was Pat Darby (on his left).

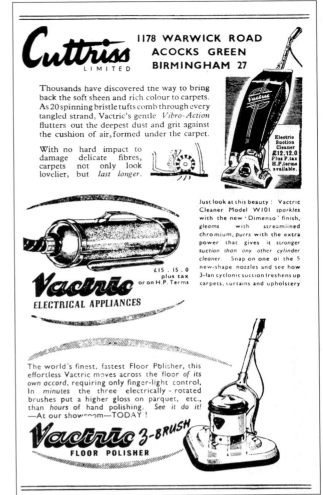

Bristol Road, with Witherford Way on the left, Selly Oak, c 1950.

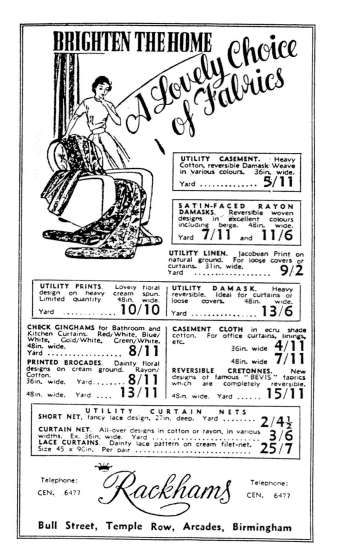
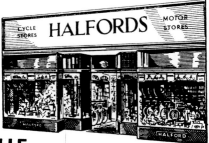

Bull Street/Temple Row, 1950.

12

Grange Road, with Eversley Road on the right, Small Heath,
5th September 1950.

SIR, — It was a great pleasure to my sister and myself to invite our friends and neighbours in to share the joys of television.

But we find it a great drain on our rations, for during intervals in the programme we usually have some refreshments, tea and biscuits, etc.

At first an occasional spoonful of tea would be presented but now it is all taken for granted. I do hope this will shake the conscience of some of these spongers, who, after all, are getting their entertainment free.

Kind Fool.

Birmingham, 13.

New John Street West/Hospital Street, Hockley, 11th September 1950.

Christmas party at Docker Bros. (paint, varnish and cellulose lacquer manufacturers),
Rotton Park Street, Ladywood, c 1950.

Women's Rally, Town Hall, 1st December 1950.

1951

Garrison Lane, Bordesley Green, 1951.

The Empire Theatre, about to be demolished after standing derelict for ten years,
Hurst Street/Smallbrook Street, 16th January 1951.

Colonnade Passage/New Street, January 1951.

16

St Michael's School netball team, Digbeth, 1951.

Queueing for coke, during the fuel shortage,
Windsor Street gasworks, Saltley, 2nd February 1951.

New Street, 30th April 1951. The films showing at the Odeon
were "Our Very Own" starring Ann Blyth and "Gambling
House" with Victor Mature.

The Civic Restaurant, run by the Council, Cannon Hill Park,
6th June 1951.

The Festival of Britain consisted of a
major exhibition and a season of
festivities to mark the centenary of the
Great Exhibition and to celebrate
postwar Britain. Held on the South
Bank of the Thames, the main features
were the Dome of Discovery and the
Skylon. Some Birmingham companies
displayed their goods.

Form 3R, Saltley Grammar School, Belchers Lane, 1951.

18   Aston Road, 1951.

Walsall Road, Great Barr, c 1951.

Factory canteen staff, H & D Churchill Ltd., Coventry Road,
South Yardley, c 1951.

Aston Brook Street/Aston Road, June 1951.

An excited family lean out of the Gould's flat to watch Princess Elizabeth pass by on her way to Victoria Square. Ledsam Street, Ladywood, 9th June 1951.

Princess Elizabeth unveils the statue of Queen Victoria, watched by the Lord Mayor, Alderman R.C. Yates.

The statue, together with that of King Edward VII, was removed from Victoria Square in March, 1950, and after renovation by the Birmingham sculptor, William Bloye, a plaster cast was made as a preliminary to a new statue being cast in bronze by H. H. Martyn & Co., of Cheltenham. The new statue was returned to Birmingham on 25th May, 1951, and resited in Victoria Square on a redesigned pedestal of reconstructed Cornish granite. The unveiling was performed by Princess Elizabeth (now Queen Elizabeth) on 9th June, 1951.

– and the finished product, for all to admire!

Birchfield Road, 19th June 1951.

Stechford Lane, Stechford, 4th July 1951.

Air display, Elmdon Airport, 9th September 1951.

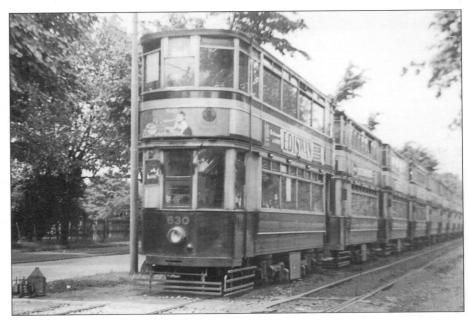

Trams are parked in Pebble Mill Road, whilst the Selly Oak depot is converted for use by motor buses, September 1951.

The White Hart winners (and supporters) of Ansells Aston Darts League, 1951.

Christmas treats at the Rock Cinema, Alum Rock Road, 1951.

Washwood Heath Road, with Thornton Road opposite, 1952.

Pershore Road, with Ivy Road in the centre, Stirchley, 1952.

Holidays for Old People

For the third year 1,000 elderly people from Birmingham will spend a holiday at Weston-super-Mare in May at a specially reduced rate. The Birmingham Council for Old People has accepted an invitation from the resort, and the arrangements are that the old people will travel by coach.

Hotels are offering a rate of £3 a week for each person. The scheme is intended for those who are more than 60 years of age and who cannot afford a holiday at present charges.

A small party will go to Paignton, whose Council for Social Service has offered to extend its scheme for a second year.

Old people interested in these holidays are asked to contact Miss W. M. Bayes at the Council for Old People at King Alfred's Place, Birmingham.

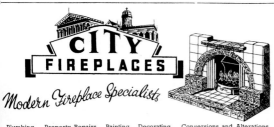
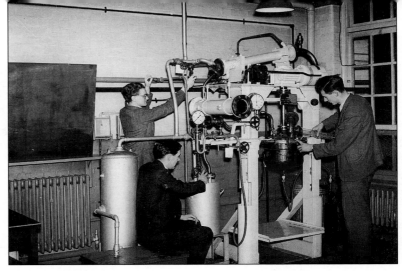

Students from the Birmingham College of Technology begin the process of plastics production, Nelson Street Schools, Sandpits, 5th February 1952. Neil Allen (right) holder of the bronze medal of the City and Guilds of London Institute, feeds the digester and looks forward to the finished product – an ashtray!

PUBLIC NOTICES

TOWN HALL,   CITY OF   BIRMINGHAM

BIRMINGHAM SYMPHONY ORCHESTRA.
Leader: NORRIS STANLEY.
CONDUCTOR: RUDOLF SCHWARZ.
THURSDAY, FEBRUARY 7, at 7 p.m.
RUTH PACKER, NORMA PROCTOR,
WILLIAM HERBERT, STANLEY MASON,
THE CITY CHOIR.
Symphony No. 102, in B Flat ....Haydn
Symphony No. 9, in D Minor (Choral)
Beethoven
No orchestra seats available for this concert.
SUNDAY, FEBRUARY 10, at 7 p.m.

JEAN POUGNET
Overture, La Scala di Seta ....Rossini
Theme and Six Diversions ....German
Violin Concerto ....Bruch
Introduction and Rondo Capriccioso
Saint-Saëns
Slavonic Dances Nos. 4, 2 and 1 ......Dvorak
Overture, The Gypsy Baron ...Johann Strauss
Tickets: Thurs., 7/6-3/-; Sun., 5/- to 3/-,
from Dale, Forty and Co. Ltd., New Street,
Birmingham, 9-5. Admission: Thursday, 2/6;
Sunday, 2/6, 1/6.

DRAPERS' CHAMBER OF TRADE
(Birmingham Branch)
"OPEN FORUM ON TRADE TOPICS"
to be held at the
BIRMINGHAM CHAMBER OF COMMERCE,
NEW STREET,
on
WEDNESDAY, FEBRUARY 13, 1952,
at 3.0 p.m.
You are Cordially Invited to attend this
Meeting and have your questions on matters
affecting the Drapery Trade answered by a
Panel of EXPERTS, consisting of
JOHN RAMAGE, O.B.E.,
Director, Association of Retail Chambers of
Trade.
MISS D. M. SMITH,
Secretary, Drapers' Chamber of Trade,
and
MR. E. WILKINSON,
Birmingham Wholesale Textile Association.
THE BIRMINGHAM PRESIDENT
(MR. C. STARK) in the Chair.

TOWN HALL, BIRMINGHAM.
FRIDAY, FEBRUARY 22, 7.45 P.M.
Ticket Man: ALAN PRIESTLEY, Ltd., Paradise
Street, 5/-, 4/-, 3/-, 2/6.
"LONDON JAZZ CLUB
COMES TO BIRMINGHAM!"
Hostess: Neva Raphaello; Music: Gallion
(London) Jazz Band; Dynamics: Denny Coffee;
Compere: H. Wilcox; Show: Best Britain Offers.

CITY OF BIRMINGHAM
MUSEUM AND ART GALLERY.
LUNCHEON-HOUR LECTURE:
"IMPRESSIONISM IN FRANCE
AND ENGLAND,"
By Dr. MARY WOODALL.
THURSDAY, FEB. 7, 1952 at 1.15 p.m.
ADMISSION FREE.

DEVONIANS IN BIRMINGHAM.
—A SOCIAL EVENING is being held on
Thursday, Feb. 14, at 7.30 p.m., at Hartfield
Crescent Schools, Acocks Green.—Particulars
from Hon. Secretary, Mrs. C. M. Short, 707,
Shirley Rd., B'ham 28. Non-members invited.

CITY OF BIRMINGHAM.
ST. MARY'S RECREATION GROUND,
LOVEDAY STREET
(Closed Burial Ground)
The PUBLIC WORKS COMMITTEE invite
tenders for the EXCAVATION AND REMOVAL
OF HUMAN REMAINS, DEMOLITION OF
SURFACE AIR RAID SHELTERS and a PUBLIC
CONVENIENCE

TOURS, DRIVES, &C.

The crowds gather to hear the proclamation of Queen Elizabeth II, Victoria Square, 8th February 1952. King George VI had died two days earlier.

OPEN-AIR AND CHURCH MEMORIAL SERVICES

15.2.52

Thousands Will Gather in Victoria Square

BIRMINGHAM to-day, in common with the whole of the country and the Empire, is paying its last tribute to King George VI at special services in the heart of the city.

An open-air memorial service is being held at 12.30 p.m. in Victoria Square, conducted by the Rector of Birmingham. The Bishop of Birmingham will pronounce the Blessing. The service will be inter-denominational and among those taking part are the Provost of Birmingham and the President of the Birmingham Free Church Federal Council. The local Jewish community will also be represented.

The singing will be led by the band of the Salvation Army and Bandmaster Langworthy will sound Last Post and Reveille.

The clergy will walk in procession from the Council House to the platform, followed by the Mace-bearer, the Town Clerk, the Lord Mayor and the Lady Mayoress. The service will last about 20 minutes, and about 10,000 copies of the order of the service will be distributed among the large congregation expected to assemble in the square.

Church Lane/Lichfield Road, Aston, 25th February 1952.

When 'Dan Archer' Was an Amateur

Harry Oakes, the "Dan Archer" of the B.B.C. serial, told an audience at the Moseley and Balsall Heath Institute that he was once a "terrified" amateur producer on the stage of the Institute.

Mr. Oakes spoke between plays at the opening session of the Birmingham and District Theatre Guild's one-act play festival. He was introduced by Mr. Robin Whitworth, chairman of the festival committee, and he recalled that it was Mr. Whitworth who, 12 years ago, first asked him to take part in a production before the "still more terrifying microphone."

The festival was opened by the Lord Mayor. The adjudicator was Mr. Leonard Hines. His general criticism of last night's performances was the players' failure to point their lines and work hard enough to get them over, but he excepted from this criticism the Highbury Students' Group, from Sutton, whose artistic handling of "The Proposal," by Tchekhov, he praised.

Albert Street, 17th March 1952.

Harry Oakes.

Preparatory work on a new island, Coventry Road/Stratford Road, Camp Hill, 1952.
Nine years later the flyover was built to ease the pressure on this area. Although originally intended to be a temporary construction, it lasted for over a quarter of a century.

Golden Hillock Road, with Armoury Road on the right, Small Heath, 28th April 1952.

Melvina Road, Vauxhall, 9th May 1952.

The Camp Service Station, Camp Hill/Warner Street, 22nd May 1952.

Slade Road, Erdington, c 1952. The Star Picture House, on the left, served the area from the beginning of the Great War until its closure on 30th August 1958.

A Sunday morning "Gammon Breakfast" run to Stourbridge for regulars of the White Hart, Aston Road, c. 1952.

The first TV detector van to hit th city's streets, Erdington, May 1952

The Deputy Lord Mayor, Alderman A.P. Smith, inspects a detachment of the crew of HMS Birmingham, Hall of Memory, 21st June 1952.

Stratford Road, with Stoney Lane on the left, Sparkbrook, 1952.

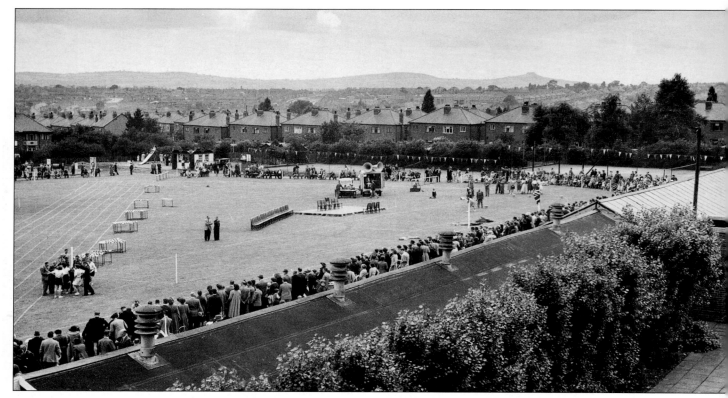

Sports' Day, Midland Red Recreation Ground, Wolverhampton Road South, Quinton, July 1952.

Rose Goodwin is proclaimed Midland Red Beauty Queen by radio star, Kenneth Horne, July 1952.

Cherrywood Road, Bordesley Green, July 1952.

IT WAS announced that Birmingham council house tenants might be allowed to buy their homes built before 1945 for as little deposit as £30. The minimum selling price for a three-bedroomed parlour-type council house was expected to be £667 to a sitting tenant.

Council houses in Birmingham are being built at £1,530 for a two-bedroomed house and £1,680 for a three-bedroomed house, the city council reported.

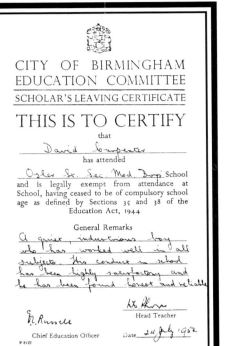

CITY OF BIRMINGHAM
EDUCATION COMMITTEE

SCHOLAR'S LEAVING CERTIFICATE

THIS IS TO CERTIFY

that

David Carpenter

has attended

Osler St. Sec. Mod. Boys' School
and is legally exempt from attendance at School, having ceased to be of compulsory school age as defined by Sections 35 and 38 of the Education Act, 1944

General Remarks

A quiet, industrious boy who has worked well in all subjects. His conduct in school has been highly satisfactory and he has been found honest and reliable.

E. Russell
Chief Education Officer

Head Teacher

Date 24 July 1952

P 8127

The tram lines start to disappear, Bristol Road, Selly Oak, 22nd August 1952.

Mott Street, Hockley, 1952.

Souvenir Programme

OF THE

CITY OF BIRMINGHAM SYMPHONY ORCHESTRA

CHARITY CONCERT

BY THE STUDENTS OF THE

Midland Accordion Centre

AND

Star Guest Artistes

AT THE

MIDLAND INSTITUTE
PARADISE STREET, BIRMINGHAM

ON

Saturday, 13th September, 1952

COMMENCING AT 7.0 P.M.

All proceeds are to be donated to the Orchestra's Endowment Fund

Programme   *Price* 6d.

The wonderfully inventive "Mr Pastry" (played by Richard Hearne) signs autographs, after completing his act, during the opening of an exhibition of Hoover products, 5th September 1952. He was appearing at the Theatre Royal, in "Blue for a Boy" at the time.

Nechells Park Road, 1952.

October 23: The Queen (Elizabeth II) yesterday opened the £2,000,000 Claerwen Dam, the culmination of a Birmingham Corporation scheme involving the building of four huge reservoirs in 59 years

Edith Pitt canvasses in the Small Heath by-election, 12th November 1952. She went on to become the MP for Edgbaston in July 1953.

Albert Road, Stechford, 1952.

Hedley Ward and his Orchestra making a very early stereophonic recording, 8th November 1952.
The engineers are J. Hickman and C.H. Banks from Witton. Stereo did not come into regular use until 1957.

Midland Red employees enjoy their annual dance, Grand Hotel, December 1952. The music was supplied by
Ronnie Hancox and his Orchestra.

Midland Counties Dairy Ltd., Bagot Street/Corporation Street, 1953.

Church Hill Road, Handsworth, 20th February 1953.

Queslett Road, Great Barr, March 1953.

Lichfield Road, with Cuckoo Road on the right, Aston, 22nd March 195

Hazelwell Road/Pershore Road, Stirchley,
March 1953.

Gravelly Lane/Mona Road, Erdington, 1953.

Evidence of drought in the city as the height post (right) is visible in the ford, Scribers Lane, Hall Green,
24th March 1953.

Max Bygraves, one of the stars of the radio programme, "Educating Archie", autographs a copy of the sheet music of "The Dummy Song" for Leslie Pike of Gillott Road, Edgbaston. Lewis's, 20th March 1953.

Unloading motor-cycles at Elmdon Airport, 6th May 1953. It was part of an experiment, conducted by the Automobile Association, to show the flexibility of transporting vehicles on behalf of holidaymakers, over relatively long distances

Staff at Joseph Lucas (Industries) Ltd., Great King Street, Hockley, c 1953.

> 1953
> BRANDED PETROL returned — pool at 4s 6d a gallon and branded, higher octane at about 4s 9d. Modification of present tax of 2s 6d a gallon expected.

Tenzing Norgay and Edmund Hilary, the first men to conquer Mount Everest, an event that captured the imagination of the whole world, May 1953.

Discarded and forlorn-looking, these chocolate machines await replacement, New Street Station, 9th April 1953.

Outside Lewis's workmen put up the decorations for the forthcoming Coronation celebrations, Corporation Street, May 1953.

Lee Bank Road, 1953.

Mr Bridgewater makes his contribution to the forthcoming events, Middleton Road, Kings Heath, 26th May 1953.

Coronation party, Oxford Street, Stirchley.

Alma Street, Aston.

Coronation Day, George Road, Erdington, 2nd June 1953.

More Coronation decorations at Joseph Lucas (gas turbine equipment) Ltd.,
Shaftmoor Lane, Hall Green, June 1953.

Jazz tenor saxophonist, Ronnie Scott, appearing in the city, 1953. In August 1991 his club opened in Broad Street.

St Margaret's Road, Ward End, June 1953.

A presentation is made during part of a Market Committee's inspection, carried out by the Lord Mayor and Lady Mayoress, Alderman and Mrs G.H. Griffith, 9th July 1953.

High Street, just before Poplar Road, Kings Heath, 1953.

Bull Street/Colmore Row, July 1953.

Steelhouse Lane, July 1953.

A presentation evening at Amie's Dance Hall, Chain Walk, Lozells, c 1953.

High Street, Aston, 6th August 1953.

Washwood Heath Road, with Asquith Road on the right, Ward End, 1953.

Car parking in the centre of the road, made possible by the removal of the old tram track to Aston. Lancaster Street, 2nd October 1953.

David Perrins and Santa, Lewis's,
Christmas 1953.

Bull Ring, 19th December 1953.

1954

The 13 Parliamentary divisions as re-constituted, in 1954, by the Boundary Commission for electoral purposes.

The annual New Year service is conducted by the Rector of Birmingham, Canon Bryan Green, in the wholesale fruit and vegetable market, 11th January 1954.

The Steam Clock, Sherborne Street/Morville Street, Ladywood, January 1954.

Alderman Mrs F. Simmons, Chairman of the Housing Management Committee and the Lord Mayor, Alderman G.H. Griffith, at the opening of the city's 100,000th council house, 218 Fairfax Road, Northfield, 29th January 1954. In the centre is the new tenant, Mrs L. Prattie.

HERBERT MANZONI, the Birmingham City Engineer and Surveyor was knighted in the New Year Honours. Sir Herbert was the best known municipal engineer in the country, and his pioneering work was a by-word outside the city.

He received the knighthood primarily for the re-planning of the city.

Moor Street Station, 1954.

High Street, with Station Road on the right, Kings Heath, 10th March 1954.

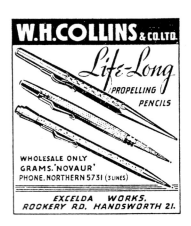

Birmingham Co-operative mobile greengrocery van, Quinton, c 1954.

Hockley Street, 1954.

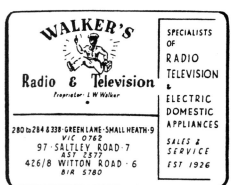

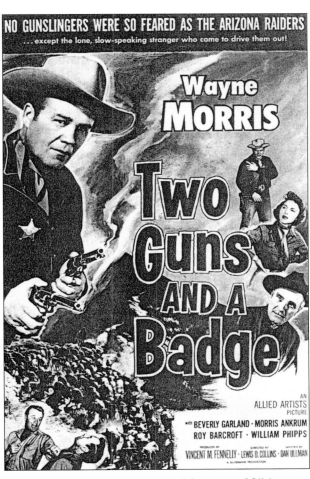

The last of the B-series Westerns, 1954.

Bull Street, looking across to Dr Johnson Passage,
31st March 1954.

Stratford Road, Sparkhill, 1954.

The irrepressible comic, Max Wall, assumes a horizontal pose, Birmingham Ice Skating Rink, Summer Hill Road, 1st April 1954. Ironically, his original bill matter read, "The Boy with the Obedient Feet"! The date seems appropriate too.

Kings Norton Grammar School for Girls, Selly Oak Road, 1954.

St George's Church, seen from St George's Place, Hockley, April 1954.

The British Industries Fair, Castle Bromwich, 8th May 1954.

The Colmore Row crossing to Snow Hill Station, 1954.

Third Avenue, with Green Lane ahead, Small Heath, May 1954.

Billy Graham, the American Evangelist (right), Odeon Cinema, 9th May 1954.

The warm spring weather encourages early paddling, Chamberlain Square, 1954.
The Central Library is in the background.

Bristol Street, with Bristol Passage in view, 2nd July 1954.

William McGeoch & Co. Ltd. (manufacturing electrical engineers and brass founders),
Coventry Road, Small Heath, c 1954.

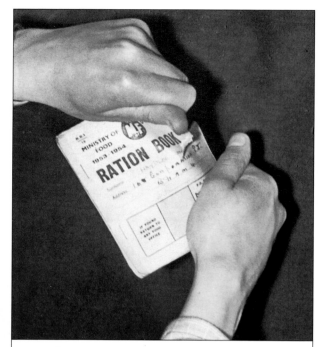

THE END of the Bread and Jam era came in 1954 as Britain's housewives tossed away the ration books that had been their life-line for over 14 years.

It was goodbye to rationing — but with a sense of gratitude. It had proved one of the war's greatest victories — share and share alike had conquered the queues, kept us alive and well.

The last night of the Proms and Rudolf Schwarz gets ready to misconduct the City of Birmingham Symphony Orchestra, Town Hall, 24th July 1954.

A popular visitor to Birmingham, with his band, Eric Delaney, recorded his big hit, "Oranges and Lemons", in August 1954. He was named "Musician of the Year" in the New Musical Express poll for 1954/55.

Castle Bromwich Cricket Club, 1954.

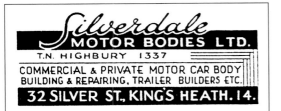

Getting ready for the Onion Fair, Serpentine fairground, Aston, 29th September 1954.

Castle Square, Weoley Castle, 5th October 1954.

Lodge Road (left) and Key Hill, from
Icknield Street, Hockley, October 1954.

FIFTY "ALEC" PANTOMIMES

Pantomime as a seasonal entertainment at the Alexandra Theatre recorded its half-century last winter. It is to that picturesque figure, Lester Collingwood, that we owe the foundation of the tradition in 1903.

Collingwood's pantomimes, like everything else he did, were hearty and flamboyant. He went all out for fun and spectacle during the seven years he ran the theatre. In the process he made several "discoveries," most famous of whom was—and is—Dorothy Ward, who made her first appearance on any stage in the "Blue Beard" of 1905. This Birmingham born star of brightest radiance had only a small part, but within a year or two she was playing principal boy—and she has played principal boy almost every season since. Another Collingwood find was Fred Barnes, a light comedian from Nechells way, who became a variety star of the first rank.

In 1910 Lester Collingwood was killed in a road accident. The Alexandra pantomime sequence continued unbroken under a new regime, that of Leon Salberg, who assumed control in 1911 and retained it until his death in 1937. Under his guidance the quality and prestige of the winter shows received considerable uplift. He engaged a succession of comedians and other principals who made themselves extremely popular in Birmingham. Among them may be quoted two fine "boys" in Victoria Carmen and Myra Hammon. In the winter of 1924-25 Leon Salberg made his own greatest personal "discovery" in Sandy Powell, then a scarcely known young comedian who, as Buttons, gave perhaps the most delightful and endearing performance of the part in my recollection.

In the 1930's stars of established position in the theatrical firmament were seen in Salberg pantomimes. Among comedians there were Georgie Wood, Billy Danvers, the Brothers Egbert, Hal Bryan, Ernie Mayne, Billy Merson, Barry Lupino and, of course, that "great dame of the British Empires," Clarkson Rose, who comes to us this season for the third time. Among boys may be named Nellie Wigley, Nora Bancroft, Nita Croft and Elizabeth French.

On Leon Salberg's death the control passed to his son Derek, who continued and accentuated the process of improvement. For his first comedy star he had the most famous of them all in George Robey. George's season in "Robinson Crusoe" began with a shock for him—and for his management—for he fell from the stage to the stalls during one of the earliest matinees and was "off" for nearly two months.

During the war the Alexandra kept its pantomimes going under the difficulties common to all, but without ever breaking the chain. Dorothy Ward herself was the first war-time "boy," with her husband Shaun Glenville as dame and Georgie Wood a third star in a sparkling cast. George Doonan, the O'Gormans, Syd and Max Harrison, Ruby Moule (today's Vanessa Lee) and Noele Gordon are among the well-known people who played here in panto for the first time while the war was on.

Since Derek Salberg's return from the army he has presented a set of pantomimes in highly ambitious artistic vein and with many outstanding personalities to adorn them. His own prize discovery is of course Norman Wisdom. Like Sandy Powell more than 20 years earlier, Norman was hardly known when he played Billy Crusoe here, and on his return as Buttons a year or two later he was still seeking fame. Today he is Britain's most lauded comedian. Another outstanding discovery was that of the Three Monarchs, now stars on T.V., stage and radio, who appeared in "Cinderella" with Norman Wisdom, and whose salary combined with his did not total that they receive on their return here this year to co-star with Clarkson Rose.

With "Aladdin," the Alexandra pantomime starts its second half-century. May his wonderful lamp light the way to success as great as the past has known. M. F. K. F.

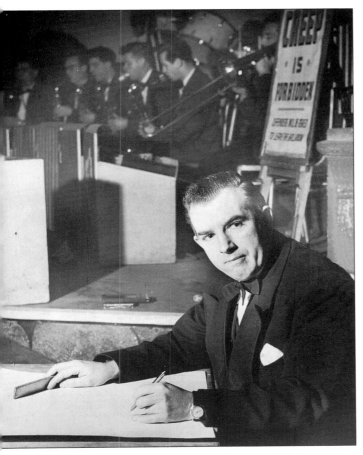

Bandleader, Cliff Deeley, Tower Ballroom, Edgbaston, 17th October 1954. It is interesting to note, from the sign behind him, that the current dance craze, "The Creep", was banned at the Tower! Mr Deeley was also a road traffic expert.

Just imagine the excitement at seeing the special train which ran to mark the centenary of the opening of the Great Western line between Snow Hill Station and Wolverhampton low level. Snow Hill, 13th November 1954.

As part of the official opening ceremony the Lord Mayor, Councillor J.R. Balmer, tours the Midland Red works, Carlyle Road, Edgbaston, 25th November 1954. The photograph was taken in the assembling shop. The 50th anniversary of the Midland Red was the same year.

1955

Bristol Street, 27th January 1955.

Regal Cinema, Soho Road/Booth Street, Handsworth, 1st February 1955. "To Dorothy a Son", starring Shelley Winters, was showing.

Drews Lane/Bromford Lane, Ward End, 1st March 1955.

Ravenshill Road, Yardley Wood, March 1955.

The Vindicatrix was a training ship for merchant seamen and over the years at least 5,000 Birmingham sailors crossed her decks. 1955. Meetings of the Vindicatrix Association are still held, on the first Wednesday in every month, at the British Servicemen's Club in Gooch Street.

Birmingham Co-operative Society Ltd., Transport Dept., Great Brook Street, Nechells, 1955.

Class 3, Elkington Street School, Aston, 1955. The teacher is Miss Cropper.

Warwick Road/Stratford Road, Sparkhill, March 1955.

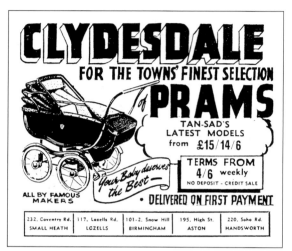

The Big Top site, viewed from the junction of New Street and High Street, 1st March 1955.

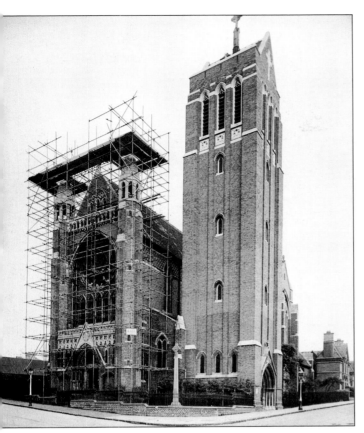

St Alban's Church, Stanhope Street/Conybere Street, Highgate, 1955.

Broad Street, with the famous Doll's Hospital on the left, sadly closed, March 1955.

Singer, Ronnie Hilton, meets the staff at one of the Midland Counties Dairies, 15th March 1955. He had hits with "No Other Love", "A Windmill in Old Amsterdam", etc.

The city's Diane Leather wins the Midland women's mile team championship for Birchfield Harriers, Salford Park, Aston, 30th May 1955.

The BBC mobile TV control unit in use for the first time, March 1955.

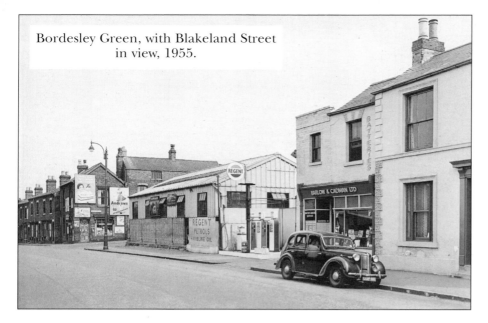

Bordesley Green, with Blakeland Street in view, 1955.

Dudley Road/Heath Street, Winson Green, 10th June 1955.

Rocky Lane, with Stretton Road on the left, Aston, 23rd June 1955.

64

Tom Dollery (second right) leads Warwickshire out for the last time as captain, Edgbaston, 20th August 1955. Amongst other successes, he had led the team successfully against the West Indian tourists in 1950 and taken the championship in 1951.

CRUISING—with music all the way—from Stourport to Worcester and back, 200 jazz fans and two bands were afloat for a day's "jam session."

Organised by Mr. Jerry Townsend, who plays trombone in the Rock Island Jazz Band, the trip was the first from Birmingham.

"We are thinking of making it an annual event," said Mr. Townsend.

The party travelled to Stourport from Birmingham by coach. Music was provided by the Rock Island Jazz Band (seen behind the dancers in the picture) and the Eagle Jazz Band.	**June 1955**

The Lord Mayor, Alderman A.L. Gibson, and officials cross the Bull Street/Corporation Street junction where the proposed pedestrian subway is to be constructed, 1955.

Birmingham's Airport at Elmdon is in the news again. The City Council has just asked the Minister of Civil Aviation to agree to enlarging the aerodrome to take trans-Atlantic services.

To Birmingham Corporation, Elmdon represents in embryo the heart of a big exporting network. But to hundreds of Midland families it means a brighter week-end, a new form of Sunday entertainment.

Eight miles, and only a six-penny bus ride from the bustle of the city-centre, on the road to Coventry, the airport today is one of the biggest single attractions in the Midlands.

Every fine Sunday during the summer hundreds of men, women and children of all ages, with their tea-flasks and picnic baskets, make a bee-line for the spacious public enclosures. In fact, say the Eastbury family, of Garretts Green Lane, Sheldon, Birmingham, who have just moved from Torquay: "The atmosphere often reminds us of a popular seaside resort."

And, it seems, eight-month-old Sharon Eastbury could not agree more, though she prefers to take her pleasures lying down.

Last year over 50,000 people paid their sixpences to watch the comings and going of aircraft at Elmdon. This year already 25,000 have paid to go in.

St John and Red Cross Hospital Library members take their service to the Women's Ward, West Heath Sanatorium, 1955.

Soho Hill, Hockley Brook, August 1955.

The paddling pool, Cannon Hill Park, August 1955.

The Queen and the Duke of Edinburgh visit Bournville, 3rd November 1955. On behalf of the Bournville community, Doris Cooke, of Cadbury's Women's Council, presents a specially designed casket.

The crowds gather in Monument Road, Ladywood, to see the Queen and the Duke of Edinburgh on their way from King Edward's School to Lucas's, Great Hampton Street, 3rd November 1955. The Royal party then went on to the opening of the new Colleges of Technology, Commerce and Art at Gosta Green.

Father Christmas travels in a vintage car, on his way to a party for 350 handicapped children, to be given at the Newtown Palace Cinema by the Cosmopolitan Bow Tie Club. Hall of Memory, Broad Street, December 1955.

Cadbury's Pensioners' Male Voice Choir, conducted by Walter Jenkins, 1955.

Bell Street, showing the Fish Market on the left, 11th December 1955.

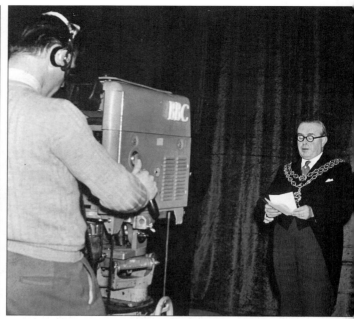

The opening of the TV studios, at Gosta Green, by the Lord Mayor, Alderman A.L. Gibson, 29th December 1955.

The finale of the first act of "Cinderella", starring Teddy Johnson and Pearl Carr (3rd right and 3rd left), Alexandra Theatre, December 1955.

1956

A New Year shock for Birmingham rate-payers today. The new valuation list has already increased the rateable value of the city by 102 per cent — from £7,386,000 to £15,848,000.

The city's current rate is 25s in the pound, equivalent to 12s. 6d. on the new valuation list. But rate-payers were warned today that the new rate is to be fixed at 18s 6d. in the pound.

Under the old valuation, this would have been 37s. in the pound.

Maryvale Road, Bournville, 3rd February 1956.

Somerville Road/Heather Road, Small Heath, 1956.

Spring Hill, with Ellen Street on the right, 1956.

Michael Crump and his mum, from Hagley Road, meet Henry Hall at a signing session for the bandleader's new autobiography, 14th February 1956.

Policewomen on duty, 1956.

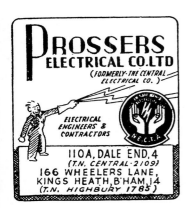

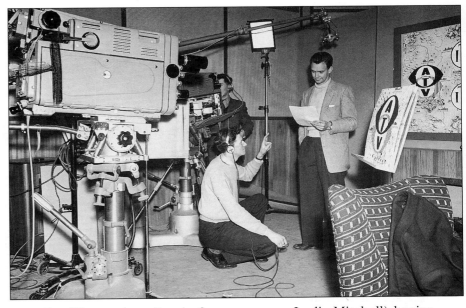

Reg Watson (standing in for announcer, Leslie Mitchell) begins
rehearsals for the first ATV programme, Aston, 7th February 1956.
He went on to produce "Crossroads" and then to devise "Neighbours"
for Australian television.

Former Soviet Premier, Georgi Malenkov, visits the GEC works, Witton,
21st March 1956. On his right is the General Manager, Mr J.J. Gracie.

Bull Street, 27th March 1956.

Bordesley Labour Working Men's Club FC, Whitmore Road, Small Heath, 1955/56.

City boxer, Johnny Mann, receives the Midland lightweight championship belt after defeating Frank Parkes, 17th April 1956.

Castle Bromwich FC, Coleshill Road, 1956.

F. A. CUP FINAL 1956

SMITH · GREEN · MERRICK · NEWMAN · BARNES · SPURDLE · DYSON · LEIVERS

ASTALL · BOYD · BADHAM · HALL · KINSEY · TRAUTMANN · PAUL · CLARKE · EWING

BROWN · MURPHY · GOVAN · HAYES · JOHNSTONE · LITTLE

74   Birmingham City lost to Manchester City, 3–1.

An excellent view, from the Big Top site, across Union Street, to Lewis's, May 1956.

Handsworth New Road, with Preston Road on the left, 1956.

Witton Road, Aston, 1956.

Station Road, Acocks Green, May 1956.

The Lord Mayor, Alderman A.L. Gibson, selects the first book to be taken out of the new public library, Brays Road, Sheldon, 14th May 1956.

John Bright Street, 1956.

John Neal (left) from Sheldon, meets his idol, the American singer, Billy Daniels, 28th May 1956. Mr Neal toured clubs as "Birmingham's Billy Daniels".

Gene Vincent, American recording star with hits such as 'Be-Bop A Lula", visited the city in 1956.

Pete Rollason's New Orleans Jazzmen (actually comprised of local musicians), The Golden Cross, Aston Cross, c 1956. The clarinet player, George Huxley (right) went on to lead his own band, becoming one of the most successful in the country. In recent times he has signed a recording contract with the American Jazzology label.

Wychall Lane, Kings Norton, 1st June 1956.

Girls from Camden Street Secondary Modern School, Spring Hill, on a trip to the Houses of Parliament, take the opportunity to photograph Dennis Howell, MP, for All Saints, 6th June 1956.

Blythe Street, Ladywood, 1956.

Soho Hill, Hockley, 19th June 1956. The cinema is the
New Palladium Picture House.

The Bishop of Birmingham, Dr J.L. Wilson, conducts the service before the foundation stone of St John the
Baptist Church is laid, Longbridge, 24th June 1956.

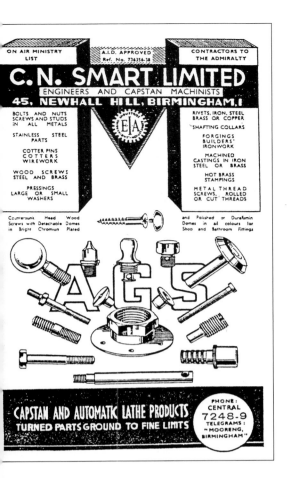

Royal Humane Society
INSTITUTED 1774.
Supported by Voluntary Contributions.
PATRON,
Her Majesty the Queen
PRESIDENT,
H.R.H. the Duke of Gloucester, K.G. &c.

At a Meeting of the Committee of the Royal Humane Society held at Watergate House, York Buildings, Adelphi, W.C.2. on the 10th day of July 1956 Present Roderick T. Hawes, Esq., T.D., in the Chair

It was Resolved Unanimously that the Honorary Testimonial of this Society, inscribed on Parchment be hereby give to

WILLIAM HENRY SCOTT

for having on the 25th May 1956 at personal risk, gone to the rescue of a boy who was unfortunately drowned in the Lifford Reservoir at King's Heath Birmingham, and whose life he gallantly assisted in attempting to save.

Workers on strike at the Austin factory, Longbridge, 3rd July 1956.

Harold Gurden (3rd from right) MP for Selly Oak, visits Mary Street Primary School, Balsall Heath, 25th September 1956.

A favourite name was missing today from the newsagents and news stands of the Midlands.
The Birmingham Gazette, originally founded as Aris's Birmingham Gazette in 1741, has ceased to publish as a separate newspaper.
Its merger with The Birmingham Post was announced on the front page of the Post which was now called "The Birmingham Post and Gazette."

Birmingham Corporation is planning to experiment with parking meters next year as a move against motorists who "hog" parking spaces for long periods.
Councillor Frank Price, chairman of the Public Works Committee said today that he believed parking meters were essential to ensure a fairer use of available street parking space.
He rejected the idea of banning cars from the city centre as "a defeatist attitude."

The lowering of the bridge to join the office and factory sections of H. Samuel Ltd., Hunters Road, Hockley, 1956.

The Carnival Queen, Barbara Green, is "chaired" into the Cinephone, shortly after its opening, Bristol Street, October 1956. The Manager, Mr R. Catton, is on the right.

Hagley Road, Edgbaston, November 1956.

Rocky Lane, near to Old Walsall Road, Hamstead,
November 1956.

Long Acre Methodist Church, Nechells, December 1956.

South African singer, Eve Boswell, tries her luck with a
Christmas cracker when she opens the new super store of
the Ten Acres and Stirchley Co-operative Society, Bristol
Road South, Northfield, 8th December 1956.

A Rock and Roll evening at the Town Hall, 1956.

The junction of Worcester Street and Station Street, from the Market Hall, January 1957.

Stafford Street/Coleshill Street, 1957.

"FINE," said Mr. Ted Hainge, "but who IS Bill Haley?"

Mr. Hainge had just been told that the cinema he manages — the Odeon — had been booked for a Birmingham concert by the high priest of rock 'n' roll.

Even now he knows about Bill Haley, Mr. Hainge says he is planning no special precautions to deal with 2,500 rock 'n' roll fans.

"Why *should* it mean trouble?" he asks.

So I went to see him . . . and heard how he tamed two teen-age gangs without violence.

It was just after the war. Mr. Hainge, just demobilised as a squadron leader, took over a London cinema where special strong-arm men were employed to keep order at week-ends.

"I soon got rid of them," he says. Instead he tried friendly persuasion.

All quiet?

THE rival gang leaders, faced with the new approach, promised not to stage battles in the cinema. Soon they would come up to Mr. Hainge, put their arms round his neck, and ask anxiously: "All quiet tonight, guv'?"

Says Mr. Hainge, whose war-time travels took him to India, Burma, China, Malaya and Siam: "I told them it was—and that I intended it to stay that way.

"You've got to be firm . . . but firm with a smile."

Tolerantly he adds: "You can't blame them too much. They grew up during the war."

Why did the gangs decide to play fair? "Perhaps they respected my grey hairs," he said. And he smiled.

In Birmingham's biggest jewel raid since the war a gang got away with £15,000 worth of loot from a Temple Row silversmiths.

By strange coincidence it was a replica of events in a Jack Hawkins movie "The Long Arm," showing in city cinemas.

In the film a gang made use of duplicate keys to reach a jeweller's safe and got away leaving as the only clue a discarded newspaper with a newsagent's pencil mark on the corner of the front page.

The thieves got into the premises of F. C. Richards, with duplicate keys and left a tattered News of the World of November 3, 1956 and the figures "182" pencilled on it.

Bill Haley, along with his Comets, after performing a sell-out concert at the Odeon, is escorted safely away, 12th February 1957. Three years before he had recorded his "Rock Around the Clock", the first record to sell a million in Britain alone. As a matter of interest, the song was featured in 14 films and recorded in 35 languages.

Leader of one of the most famous big bands of the time, Count Basie (left) meets his fans, Town Hall, 20th April 1957.

St Laurence Church, Church Road, Northfield, 1957.

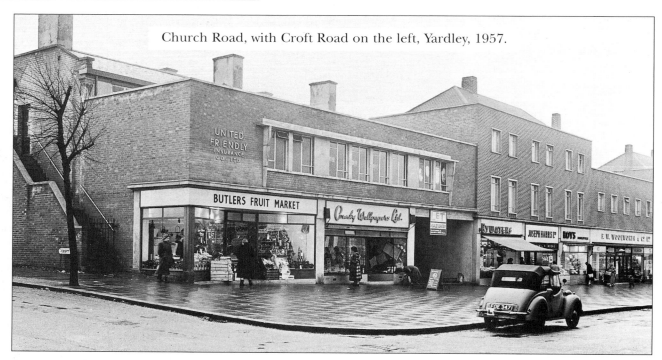

Church Road, with Croft Road on the left, Yardley, 1957.

Albert Road, Stechford, April 1957.

The Queen Mother gets a royal reception, Hunters Road, Hockley, 2nd May 1957. It is interesting to look back to page 82 to see this bridge being lowered into position.

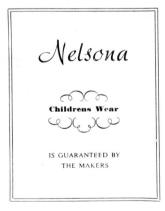

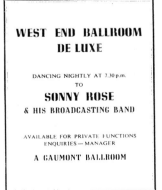

The Queen Mother arrives at Kynoch Works, Witton,
2nd May 1957.

Aston Villa train on milk supplied by Midland Counties Dairies –
and it does the trick – they beat Manchester United 2–1, at Wembley,
to win the Cup, 4th May 1957.

Lower Tower Street/Newtown Row,
4th July 1957.

Limberlost Café, Butlers Road, Handsworth, 1957.

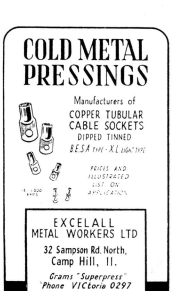

The Queen and the Duke of Edinburgh on their way to the Scouts' Jubilee
Jamboree at Sutton Park, 3rd August 1957.

Selly Park Girls' School, Pershore Road, c 1957.

The Vikings Skiffle Group, Catherine Street, Aston, 1957.

Sarah Street/Lower Dartmouth Street, Bordesley, 9th October 1957.

The Lord Mayor, Alderman J.J. Grogan, bowls the first wood on the new indoor green at Saltley Baths, 19th October 1957.

Woodthorpe Road, Kings Heath, 1957.

Redevelopment in Hurst Street, leading up to the work taking place on Smallbrook Ringway, 1st November 1957. The Locarno was built to the right of the Empire Fish Restaurant. In its transition from dance hall to discotheque it has undergone several name changes and is currently known as Pulse.

PRINTING IN BIRMINGHAM
FOR 136 YEARS
FIVE GENERATIONS IN CITY COMPANY

ONE hundred and thirty-six years ago Benjamin Hudson founded the family firm of Hudson & Son by setting up his first printing press at 18, Bull Street. The son of a Lutterworth baker, Benjamin had been indentured into the printing craft in 1788, his father having paid the princely sum of £99 19s. 0d. for the privilege of apprenticing his son for seven years. In those early days Number 18, Bull Street, was primarily a bookshop, but leaflets, tracts and stationery were printed, and papers, pamphlets and the like distributed.

Before *The Post*

Long before *The Birmingham Post* was even thought of, the news and views of the day were circulated in the form of news sheets and pamphlets and these were a constant source of trouble to the Government of the time. A law was enacted "*for the better preventing of treasonable and seditious practices*" and under this Act all printers had to be registered and vouched for. In 1831 Benjamin Hudson was duly registered and his near business neighbour Mr. B. H. Cadbury attested his

signature. After 126 years Hudsons are no longer near neighbours of the great Cadbury firm but they are proud to be entrusted with much of their work. It is a far cry to the days when Hudson & Son printed religious tracts and political leaflets that were so much a part of the free and advanced thinking of the Birmingham of this period, for to-day catalogue and colour printing of the highest quality is more in their line of work.

The Bull Street premises soon became too small for a growing concern and in 1876 new and improved quarters were found in Dale End. However a new building was soon needed and Edmund Street was just being developed. "This will be an important street one day," was the comment made by William Hudson, but he died in 1881 and his widow, helped by their sons Reginald and Percy, carried the new work through.

Edmund Street . . .

On March 27th, 1883, it was announced in the *Mail* that the firm had moved to their "Newly erected and Most Commodious Premises" and the first part of the new works

in Edmund Street was completed. Between 1883 and the first Great War there were frequent extensions of premises. At first there had been a "pub" and a stables at the back of the works, the former a popular feature with employees, but these were pulled down and new works built to meet the growing demands for print.

. . . and Livery Street

A landmark in the firm's history came in 1899 when the property known as Medova Buildings, on the corner of Edmund Street and Livery Street, was purchased and became the offices and the stationery shop; the firm continued to prosper and expand. Mr. Reginald Hudson became President of the Birmingham Master Printers and held this office during the first World War. Together with his brother Percy Hudson and his partner, Arthur Vaughton, they bought the business of W. Rickman King and continued to build on the Edmund Street site until they had a factory of over forty-thousand square feet and employed some two hundred people.

A natural outcome of this growth was the formation of the present Company of

Hudson & Son Ltd. in 1934. During the second World War the works escaped miraculously a series of minor hits and fires which, but for the devotion of the employees, would have razed the place to the ground.

Still Growing

Since the war progress has been even more marked with great strides in plant modernisation. In 1954 the old established Birmingham company of Buckler & Webb Ltd. was acquired. The Group's products continued to expand and improve and in a recently organised national exhibition of "A 100 Good Catalogues" no less than five came from their works. The Company claim that they have the best technical skill and some of the finest printing machinery in Europe, assets which are in demand by many of the greatest manufacturing industries.

In the past ten years Hudson & Son Ltd has more than doubled in size and they do not propose to rest on their laurels. They hope that by giving quality and service they will repeat the performance in years to come.

Jubilee celebration for the 7th Birmingham Company of the Boys' Brigade and old boys, Watford Road Congregational Church, Cotteridge, 1957.

New Bond Street/Coventry Road, Camp Hill, January 1958.

Worcester Street, with New Street top left, 8th January 1958.

Ermington Crescent, Castle Bromwich, 1958.

Bristol Road South, Northfield, 1958.

Originally a coaching house, this property is earmarked for demolition, High Street, Erdington, 1958.

Aston Villa's mascot, "The Villain", greets Stanley Matthews, on his birthday, as he takes the field with the Blackpool team, Villa Park, 1st February 1958.

Tony Hancock, appearing in his first straight television role in the BBC's "The Government Inspector", 9th February 1958.

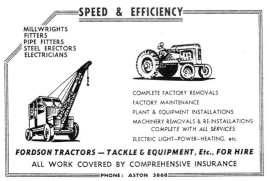

Henry's, about to be demolished, makes way for Littlewoods, High Street/Martineau Street, February 1958.

The Laura Dixon Formation Dancing Team, February 1958.

Betty Fox with some of her pupils, March 1958. She was the best-known teacher of tap and modern ballet in the city and numbered, amongst her many students, Billy Dainty and Alton!

The Lady Mayoress, Mrs J.J. Grogan, visits St Andrew's Primary School, Small Heath, 6th March 1958.

The stay that stays put

A NEW type of collar stay, permanently sewn in and claimed to be unbreakable, is now being used in shirts on sale in Britain. Trustays, as they are called, are made of plastic and rubber; it is likely that they will soon be adapted for use in strapless bras, dresses and girdles.

More than 80,000 pairs of the new-type stay are being made every week, and the manufacturers are extending to keep up with the demand.

As part of the Sunday Mercury's "Secret Ambition" series, Barbara Boffey, Carole King and Janice Williams, meet Canadian teenage singing sensation (and the first "pop" millionaire) Paul Anka, 23rd March 1958. He went on to write the enormous hit, "My Way" and to remain a star into the nineties.

A fan of the stars, Phyllis Burton, (centre) meets two of her idols, singers, Yana and Edmund Hockridge, backstage at the Hippodrome, 27th March 1958.

Broad Street/Bishopsgate Street, 1958.

Cuckoo Road, Nechells, 1958.

Church Road, Yardley, 1958.

Five Ways, taken from Hagley Road, April 1958.

St Stephen's Road/Pershore Road, Stirchley, April 1958.

A flatted factory, Dartmouth Street, 18th April 1958.

Danny King and the Dukes, 1958. Locally-based but working internationally.

The concert to be given by Rock and Roll star, Jerry Lee Lewis, is cancelled due to the scandal surrounding his child-bride, Odeon, New Street, 28th May 1958.

A suitably-attired Teddy boy and his partner at an all-night jazz ball at the Town Hall, 1958.

The Saracen's Head, Kings Norton Green, 1958.

Something *NEW* in motoring

The *Scootacar*

... AND IT'S 100% BRITISH

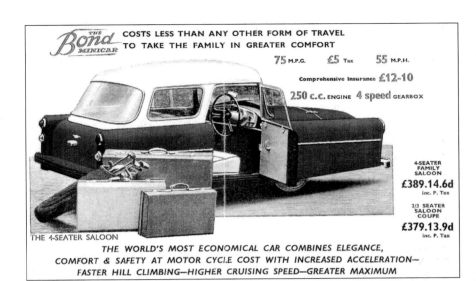

The *Bond* MINICAR COSTS LESS THAN ANY OTHER FORM OF TRAVEL TO TAKE THE FAMILY IN GREATER COMFORT

75 M.P.G.   £5 Tax   55 M.P.H.

Comprehensive Insurance £12-10

250 C.C. ENGINE   4 speed GEARBOX

4-SEATER FAMILY SALOON
£389.14.6d
inc. P. Tax

2/3 SEATER SALOON COUPE
£379.13.9d
inc. P. Tax

THE 4-SEATER SALOON

THE WORLD'S MOST ECONOMICAL CAR COMBINES ELEGANCE, COMFORT & SAFETY AT MOTOR CYCLE COST WITH INCREASED ACCELERATION—FASTER HILL CLIMBING—HIGHER CRUISING SPEED—GREATER MAXIMUM

THE NEW *HEINKEL* DE LUXE CRUISER

£403-6-6
(including Purchase Tax)

family car performance
motor cycle economy

VLO 868

RUSH PRINTED HAND-OUT

AND NOW THE FULL

4-5 seat

Isetta

600

Isetta WORLD'S CHEAPEST CARS TO BUY AND RUN

DE LUXE CRUISER *THE ECONOMY CAR* FOR BUSINESS OR PLEASURE

*H*ERE is a car that will take two adults and two children—or plenty of luggage. It will take you where you want in comfort and will travel approx. 90 miles on a gallon of petrol. The sturdy 4-stroke engine will tackle hills and give steady performance in traffic. There are four gears (and reverse) a press button starter, and a heater. The windows give wonderful visibility and the sunshine roof folds back at a touch from the driver's seat.

Because the Heinkel Cruiser can be parked almost anywhere it is becoming more and more popular with those working in towns and with housewives who live some way from shops and schools.

Here is a car you can afford to own, whose good looks attract attention everywhere and with a built-in dependability which will carry you to country, coast or town, safely and speedily. The Heinkel Cruiser is pleasant economy!

VLO 868

THE NEW DE LUXE IS MORE POWERFUL... AND IT COSTS LESS

Electro Magnets Ltd., Bond Street (off Constitution Hill)
18th June 1958.

Turner Bros. Ltd. (press tool manufacturers)
Cliveland Street, 18th June 1958.

THIS IS THE 250,000th VEHICLE PRODUCED at LONGBRIDGE SINCE AUGUST·1957

17th July 1958.

THEATRES 24.7.58 CINEMAS

ALEXANDRA THEATRE

Evgs. 7.15 (Sat 5.25 and 8) Mat Wed. 2.30.
Derek Salberg's Repertory Company
THE WALTZ OF THE TOREADORS
Comedy of Love and Marriage by Jean Anouilh.
28th: DRY ROT.
Box Office 10—7.15. MID 1231.

REPERTORY THEATRE

8th July — 2nd August
"THE POTTING SHED" by Graham Greene. Evenings 7.0. Matinees Wednesdays and Saturdays, 2.30 Usual Agents. Box Office (MIDland 2471) open 10.0 a.m.—7.30 p.m.

SHAKESPEARE Memorial Theatre

1958 SHAKESPEARE SEASON. Today: "Hamlet." Tom: "Pericles." Book Now! Civic Radio Service, 27b Paradise St. (MID 0021). Evgs. 7.30. Mats.: Thurs. Sat. 2.30.

BIRMINGHAM HIPPODROME

Twice Nightly 6.15 and 8.30.
VIC DAMONE
Great American Recording Star.
28th: Diana Decker. Eddie Gray. Arthur English. Max & Harry Nesbitt. Herschel Henlere.
Now bkg.: DAVID WHITFIELD in London Palladium ROBINSON CRUSOE. (Opens Dec. 24th).
Box Office 10-9. MID 2576/7. Agencies

ASTON HIPPODROME
ASTON HIPPODROME

6.20 — 8.30. Twice Nightly.
Phone AST 2341. B.O. 10—7.
The new American Strip-Tease Revue
"NITE LIFE NEW YORK"
Star Cast. Novelty Scenes. Laughter unlimited. See the Nude Ranch, and play the Strip Quizz.

WINDSOR THEATRE
BEARWOOD

Mon.-Fri. 7.30 Sat. 6.15 and 8.30.
FAMOUS PLAYERS
"GIVE ME YESTERDAY"
28th: SWEET FANNY ADAMS.
Aug. 4th: DRY ROT."
Box Office 10—8 BEA 2244. Free Park

ARENA THEATRE

CANNON HILL PARK
7.15 Today "The Diary of Anne Frank." Friday and Saturday: "The Reluctant Debutante." Monday and Tuesday: "The Diary of Anne Frank" B.O. 9—6. Civic Radio, Paradise Street. MID 0021.

PARKS SUMMER SHOWS

LIGHTWOODS
Today 7.30 Search for Stars. Friday 3.0 Punch and Judy. 7.30 "Stars of Today. Saturday 3.0 Ann Harris Juveniles. 7.30 "Larks in the Parks."
SPARKHILL
Today 7.30 Search for Stars Winners. Friday 3.0 "Babes in the Wood" panto. 7.30 "Variety Parade." Saturday 3.0 Punch and Judy, 7.30 "Capers of 1958."
WARD END
MON. 3 and 7.30: DAVID BERGLAS in "Radio and TV. Stars."

COVENTRY

THE COVENTRY THEATRE

Evgs. 7.30 (Sat. 5 and 8).
MOSCOW STATE VARIETY THEATRE
28th: Diana Dors. Aug. 4th: Beryl Reid. Earle & Vaughan, Bernard Miles. 11th: John Slater in THE ENTERTAINER. 18th: FREE AS AIR Bkg: 21st Birthday Show (with DAVID WHITFIELD and "Robin Hood" (with JEWEL & WARRISS) Each Mon. (exc. Bank Holiday) two seats for price of one.
Box Office 10—8 COV 3141. Agencies

WEDNESBURY

WEDNESBURY HIPPODROME

This Week
H. J. Barlow presents the Wednesbury Repertory Company in the favourite thriller
"THE SHOP AT SLY CORNER"
by Edward Percy
Nightly 7.30. Fri. 8.0, Sat. 6.0 & 8.15
Box Office (WED 0634) open 10—8

MID 6101 **ODEON** NEW ST Cont. 10 a.m
William HOLDEN, Sophia LOREN, Trevor HOWARD, in
THE KEY (A)
CINEMASCOPE
At 11.5 a.m., 2.10, 5.15 and 8.25 p.m
RIVERS OF TIME (U)
in Eastman Colour.
At 10.20 a.m., 1.20, 4.25 and 7.30 p.m
LICENSED RESTAURANT Open to the Public 10.30 a.m.—8.30 p.m

MID 1761 **CINEPHONE** Bristol Street
BRITISH PREMIERE OF
The Most Daring Film yet . . .
JUVENILE PASSION (X)
(Eng sub-titles).
Frank . . Outspoken . Sex in the East at 1.50, 4.20, 6.50, 9.20
also
ELYSIA (A)
Cert. (Birmingham)
Actually Filmed in a Nature Camp at 1.0, 3.25, 5.55 8.25
Coffee Lounge open 10.30am—11.30pm

GAUMONT
Steelhouse Lane. CEN 3014.
Continuous 1.0. L.C. Prog. 7.20.
Clark Gable, Burt Lancaster.
RUN SILENT, RUN DEEP (u)
Screened at 2.35, 5.45, 8.55.
Neil McCallum, Susan Beaumont, William Hartnell.
ON THE RUN (a)
Screened at 1.05, 4.15, 7.25.

WEST END
BIRMINGHAM
HURRY! Must Finish August 9.
Cecil B. De Mille's Production of
THE TEN COMMANDMENTS (U)
In Technicolor and VistaVision
Twice Daily, 1.45 p.m. and 6.40 p.m Sundays 5.30 p.m.
ALL SEATS BOOKABLE IN ADVANCE NOW from the Theatre Box Office. Open daily 10 a.m.—8 p.m. except Sundays. Phone: MID 1188.
(Postal Bookings Accepted) and at Lewis's Ltd.
Prices: 3/6, 5/6, 7/6 and 10/6.

Today Cont. 10.15 A.B.C. **FORUM** MID 4549
GEORGE BAKER : SYLVIA SYMS
PETER ARNE : MARIUS GORING
THE MOONRAKER
Technicolour (U)
Showing at 11.50, 2.55, 5.55 & 9.0
JOHN ERICSON, LOLA ALBRIGHT
OREGON PASSAGE (U)
Cinemascope, De Luxe Color.
Showing at 10.15, 1.15, 4.15 & 7.20

Cont. 12.15 A.B.C. **BRISTOL** Bristol Rd. CAL 1904
VAN HEFLIN : TAB HUNTER
KATHERINE GRANT
GUNMAN'S WALK (A)
CinemaScope Technicolor
2.00, 5.25, 8.55
ELI WALLACH : ROBERT KEITH
THE LINE UP (A)
12.25 3.45, 7.10

Theatre MID 1292 **FUTURIST** Cafe MID 1579
Retained 3rd Week
MAN HUNT (u)
Eastman Colour — Starring
DON MURRAY : DIANE VARSI
Chill Wills : Dennis Hopper
Screened at 1.0, 3.30, 6.0, 8.30
A 20th Century Fox
CINEMASCOPE

Let's go to the Pictures CINEMATOGRAPH EXHIBITORS' ASSOCIATION *Denotes 6-day Programme

ABC ADELPHI, Hay Mills VIC 1208 Joel McCrea, **The Tall Stranger** (u); Terry Dene, **The Golden Disc** (u). Sun: **The Dam Busters** (u).

ALBION, NEW INNS, HANDSWORTH Victor Mature, **NO TIME TO DIE** (u); Edmond O'Brien, **WORLD WAS HIS JURY** (u).

ABC ALHAMBRA, Moseley Rd. VIC 2826. Joel McCrea, **The Tall Stranger** (u) C/Scope; **The Golden Disc** (u). Sun: It's Magic (a).

APOLLO, Tyburn Road — ERD 0834 Tab Hunter, **Hell Bent for Glory** (a); G. Montgomery, **Black Patch** (a). Sun: Big House U.S.A. (a).

ATLAS STECHFORD —— STE 2206 **GRAND RE-OPENING SUNDAY, JULY 27**. Ga. at 3.45 p.m.

BEACON —— GREAT BARR **Isle of Levant** (a) Col. **The Wic...** Go to Hell (x). Adults only. Sun: It Came From Outer Space (u).

BEAUFORT — WASHWOOD HEATH **Rodan** (x); Robert Mitchum, **Build My Gallows High** (a). Adults only. Sun: Back to God's Country (a).

BIRCHFIELD, Perry Barr BIR 4333 Cont 2.0: **The Quiet American** (a); **Toughest Gun in Tombstone** (u). Sun: Gunman in the Streets (a).

CAPITOL —— WARD END Nat King Cole, **ST. LOUIS BLUES** (u); John Derek, **HIGH HELL** (a). Sunday: Rails into Laramie (u).

CARLTON, Sparkbrook — SOU 0861 Joel McCrea, **The Tall Stranger** (u) C/Scope; **The Golden Disc** (u). Sun: The Blazing Forest (u) Tech.

CLIFTON —— GREAT BARR **Seven Hills of Rome** (u) (Sat. 3.5), 5.50, 8.30; **The Magic Lamp** (u). Sun: Rails into Laramie (u).

CORONET, Small Heath — VIC 0420 Glenn Ford **The Sheepman** (u); J. Mason, **Cry Terror** (x). Adults only. Sun: Counterfeit Plan (a).

CROWN, Ladywood (ABC) EDG 1123 Josephine Douglas, Dickie Valentine, Lonnie Donegan, **6.5 SPECIAL** (u). Sun.: Canyon River (u).

ABC EDGBASTON —— EDG 3272 Mario Lanza, **Seven Hills of Rome** (u); **The Devil's Pass** (u). L.P. 7.15. Sun: The First Texan (u).

ELITE, Handsworth —— NOR 0665 John Gregson, Muriel Pavlow, **Rooney** (u); **Running Target** (u). Sun: Turn the Key Softly (a).

EMPRESS, Sutton (ABC) SUT 2363 Marlon Brando, Montgomery Clift, **The Young Lions** (a) C/S. Sun: **Dracula** (x). Adults only.

ERA CINEMA, BORDESLEY GREEN John Gregson, **Rooney** (u); **The Man From Bitter Ridge** (u) Tech. Sun: Street of Shadows (a).

ESSOLDO, Longbridge —— PRI 2471 **THE YOUNG LIONS** (a) C/Scope 1.35, 4.40, 7.50. Last performance 7.30. Sunday: The Sea Chase (u).

ESSOLDO Quinton —— WOO 2562 Marlon Brando, **THE YOUNG LIONS** (a) 1.30, 4.30, 7.30. Sunday: Border River (u).

GAIETY, Coleshill St. (ABC) CEN 6649. V. Mature **China Doll** (a); Joel McCrea, **Fort Massacre** (u). Sun: The Brave & the Beautiful. (a).

GAUMONT, Smethwick — SME 0950 L. Turner, **Another Time, Another Place** (a); **Run for Cover** (u). L.P. 7.0. Sun: Ten Little Niggers (a).

GRAND, Alum Rock Rd. — EAS 0471 William Holden, Kim Novak **PICNIC** (a) C Scope Col. Sun: My Sister Eileen (u)

GRANGE, Small Heath — VIC 0434 Susan Strasberg, **Stage Struck** (u); Diana Dors, **I Married A Woman** (u). Sun: Chicago Syndicate (a)

GROVE CINEMA, Dudley Rd. SME 0343. Henry Fonda, **Stage Struck** (u); Diana Dors, **I Married A Woman** (u). Sun. Shotgun (a).

ABC IMPERIAL, Moseley Rd. CAL 2283. **The Happiest Days of Your Life** (u); **They Who Dare** (u). L.P. 7.0. Sun: The Kentuckian (u).

KING'S NORTON —— KIN 1079 **Another Time, Another Place** (a); **The Naked Jungle** (u) L.P. 7.0 Sun: Girls in Prison (a).

KINGSTON, Small Heath VIC 2629 **Isle of Levant** (u); **The Width of the Pavement** (x). Adults only Sun: Counterfeit Plan (a).

KINGSWAY —— HIG 1352 Nat King Cole, **St. Louis Blues** (u) 2.5, 5.20, 8.40; **High Hell** (a). L.P 7.0. Sun: Chicago Syndicate (a).

LUXOR —— CAL 2008 Robert Mitchum, **Thunder Road** (a); D. Walsh, **Woman of Mystery** (a). Sun: Sitting Bull (u)

LYRIC —— PARADE J. Powell, **Seven Brides for Seven Brothers** (u); **Double Fraud** (u). Sun: Big House U.S.A. (a).

MAJESTIC —— BEARWOOD Richard Todd, Joan Rice, **Robin Hood and His Merrie Men** (u); C. Rafferty, **Walk Into Paradise** (u).

MAYFAIR —— PERRY COMMON Glenn Ford, **The Sheepman** (u); James Mason, **Cry Terror** (a). Sun: The Stars Are Singing (u).

MAYPOLE, King's Heath MAY 2051 **Rodan** (x) 5.54, 8.50; **Rider From Tucson** (u). Adults only. L.P. 7.14. Sun: Rancho Notorious (a) Tech.

NEWTOWN PALACE —— ASTON **The Quiet American** (a); **Toughest Gun in Tombstone** (u). Sun: City Beneath the Sea (u) Tech.

NORTHFIELD CINEMA —— PRI 1463 John Gregson, **ROONEY** (u); **YANK IN ERMINE** (u) L.P. 7.10. Sun: Trouble in Store (u).

OAK, Selly Oak (ABC) — SEL 0139 Marlon Brando, **The Young Lions** (a) C Scope 1.10, 4.25, 7.40. Sun: World Without End (a) Tech. C/S.

ODEON, Blackheath —— BLA 1036 **THUNDER ROAD** (a) 2.35, 5.45, 8.50; **A WOMAN OF MYSTERY** (a) 4.20, 7.25, L.P. 7.25.

ODEON —— KINGSTANDING **GIDEON'S DAY** (a) 2.25, 5.43, 9.0; **GOING STEADY** (a) 3.56, 7.15, L.P. 7.10. Sun: Chicago Syndicate (a)

ODEON —— PERRY BARR Cont. 2.10: **Rodan** (x); **Rachel and The Stranger** (a) Adults only. Sun: Pearl of the South Pacific (u).

ODEON —— SHIRLEY Henry Fonda, **Stage Struck** (u); **I Married A Woman** (u). L.P. 7.5. Sun: Five Against the House (a).

ODEON —— SUTTON **Rodan** (x) 2.40, 5.55, 9.5; **Back to Bataan** (a). Adults only. L.P. 7.10. Sun: Teacher's Pet (u) V Vis.

ODEON, Warley —— BEA 1549 Henry Fonda, **Stage Struck** (u); **I Married a Woman** (u). L.P. 7.5. Sunday: War Arrow (u).

OLTON CINEMA —— ACO 0593 Max Bygraves, **Charley Moon** (u); **See How They Run** (u). Sun: Black Dakotas (x). Adults only.

OLYMPIA, Ladypool Rd. — VIC 0124 Randolph Scott, **SEVEN MEN FROM NOW** (u); **THE D.I.** (u). Sun: Just For You (u) Tech.

ABC ORIENT, ASTON — NOR 1615 **Seven Hills Of Rome** (u) 2.40, 5.40, 8.40; **The Devil's Pass** (u) L.P. 7.25. Sun: The Burning Hills (u).

PALACE, Erdington (ABC) ERD 1623 Marlon Brando, Montgomery Clift, **The Young Lions** (a) C/S L.P. 7.15. Sunday: Trouble Shooter (a).

PALLADIUM, Hockley (ABC) NOR 0380. Jack Hawkins, **Gideon's Day** (a); **Going Steady** (a). Sun: Geo. Montgomery, Canyon River (u).

ABC PAVILION, Stirchley KIN 1241 **Seven Hills of Rome** (u); **The Devil's Pass** (u). L.P. 7.20. Sun: Rock, Rock Rock (u).

ABC PAVILION, Wylde Green ERD 0224. **Seven Hills of Rome** (u) Tech. 2.30, 5.35, 8.40 **The Devil's Pass** (u). L.P. 7.15. Sun.: Inferno (a) Tech.

PICCADILLY, Sparkbrook (ABC) VIC 1688. Marlon Brando, Montgomery Clift, **The Young Lions** (a) C.S. Sun: Kiss Me Deadly (a).

PICTURE HOUSE, Aston Cross (ABC) EAS 0430. **Seven Days' Leave** (u); D. O'Keefe, **Leonard Man** (a) Sun: The Big Combo (a).

PLAZA, Stockland Green ERD 1048 **Rodan** (x) 2.05, 5.35, 9.15; **Tension at Table Rock** (u). Adults only Sun: Mississippi Gambler (u).

PRINCES Smethwick —— SME 0221 David Tomlinson, **Up the Creek** (u); **The Lone Ranger** (u) Col. Sunday: Old Yeller (u).

ABC REGAL, Handsworth NOR 1801 Mario Lanza, **Seven Hills of Rome** (u); **The Devil's Pass** (u). L.P. 7.25. Sun: The Big Knife (a).

RIALTO, Hall Green —— SPR 1270 Nat King Cole, **St. Louis Blues** (u); John Derek, **High Hell** (a). L.P. 7.10. Sun: The Brain Machine (a)

ABC RITZ, Bordesley Green VIC 1070 Joel McCrea, **The Tall Stranger** (u); Terry Dene, **The Golden Disc** (u). Sun: The Dam Busters (u).

ABC ROBIN HOOD — HALL GREEN Mario Lanza, **Seven Hills of Rome** (u); **The Devil's Pass** (u). L.P 7.25. Sunday: The Gun Runner (a).

ROCK CINEMA —— ALUM ROCK Eddie Albert, **Orders To Kill** (a); **Notorious Mr. Monks** (a). Sunday: Dangerous Mission (a) Tech.

ABC ROYALTY, Harborne HAR 1619 Mario Lanza, **Seven Hills of Rome** (u); **Devil's Pass** (u). L.P. 7.20. Sun: Rock, Rock, Rock (u).

RUBERY CINEMA —— RUBERY 193 Ray Milland, **The Safecracker** (a) 5.45, 9.0; **Saddle the Wind** (a). LP 7.20. Sun: Go Man, Go (u).

SHELDON CINEMA —— SHE 2158 Susan Strasberg, **Stage Struck** (u); Diana Dors, **I Married A Woman** (u). L.P. 7.10. Sun: Mohawk (a).

SOLIHULL —— SOL 0398 John Mills, Richard Attenborough, **DUNKIRK** (u). Full Support. Sunday: Sitting Bull (u).

STAR CINEMA —— EAS 0461 Robert Mitchum, **Thunder Road** (a); Dermot Walsh, **Woman of Mystery** (a). Sun: The Ringer (a).

TIVOLI —— COVENTRY ROAD Nat King Cole, **St. Louis Blues** (u); John Derek, **High Hell** (a). Sun: The Golden Blade (u).

TRIANGLE, Gooch St. — CAL 1060 Tommy Steele, **The Duke Wore Jeans** (u); **Double Fraud** (u). Sun: Man Behind the Gun (u).

ABC TUDOR, King's Heath HIG 1161 **CHICAGO CONFIDENTIAL** (a); **The Iron Sheriff** (u). L.P. 7.20. Sun: Rookies Come Home (u).

TYSELEY, Warwick Rd. — ACO 0133 Tommy Steele, **The Duke Wore Jeans** (u); **The Flying Scot** (u) Sunday: French Line (u).

VICTORIA —— EAS 0479 Victor Mature, Li Li Hua, **China Doll** (a); **Fort Massacre** (a) Col Sun: Tropic Zone (u) Tech.

VILLA CROSS —— NOR 0607 Nat King Cole, **St. Louis Blues** (u); John Derek, **High Hell** (a). Sun: Too Late For Tears (a).

WALDORF —— SPARKBROOK Fred MacMurray, **Gun for a Coward** (u) C/Scope; **Tammy** (u) C/Scope. Sun: Crossed Swords (u).

WARWICK —— ACOCKS GREEN Henry Fonda, **Stage Struck** (u); **I Married A Woman** (u). Sun: Hurricane Smith (u) Tech.

WEOLEY, Weoley Castle — HAR 1490 Gene Kelly, **Anchors Aweigh** (u) Tech.; **Nothing But Trouble** (u). Sun: Sabre Jet (u).

WINSON GREEN —— NOR 1790 Richard Todd, **Chase a Crooked Shadow** (u); **No Place to Hide** (u). Sun.: Smiley Gets A Gun (u).

WEST BROMWICH CINEMAS

IMPERIAL —— WES 0192 Henry Fonda, **Stage Struck** (u); Diana Dors, **I Married A Woman** (u). Sun: Rails Into Laramie (u).

KING'S West Bromwich — WES 0030 Nat King Cole, **St. Louis Blues** (u); John Derek, **High Hell** (a). Sun: Teacher's Pet (u). V. Vis.

QUEEN'S, West Bromwich WES 0351 **The Amazing Colossal Man** (a); Rod Cameron, **Escapement** (a) Sun: Smiley Gets A Gun (u).

REX CINEMA —— WED 0182 **Gunfight at the O.K. Corral** (a); **You're a Trooper** (u). Sunday: Botany Bay (a).

STONE CROSS —— STO 2141 **THE NAKED TRUTH** (u). **SIMON AND LAURA** (a) Col. On Stage: Variety Showboat 8.12 p.m.

ABC TOWER —— WES 1210 Natalie Wood, G. Kelly **Marjorie Morningstar** (u); **Night Crossing** (a). Sun: Dam Busters (a).

DUDLEY PORT CINEMA

ALHAMBRA, Dudley Port — TIP 1406 Frank Sinatra **Pal Joey** (u) Tech. **The Parson and the Outlaw** (a) Mon. Next: Time for Action (a).

GREAT BRIDGE CINEMA

PALACE, Great Bridge — TIP 1595 Louis Jourdan, **Dangerous Exile** (a) Tech.; Nat King Cole, **Musical Story** (u) Sun: Gun Belt (u).

LANGLEY GREEN CINEMA

REGENT, Langley Green BRO 1120 Deborah Kerr, **Bonjour Tristesse** (a); **Escape from San Quentin** (a). Sun: The Grace Moore Story (u).

WEDNESBURY CINEMAS

PALACE —— WEDNESBURY I. Carmichael, **Happy is the Bride** (u); **Tall Trouble** (u). L.P. 7.25 Sunday: Timeslip (a).

RIALTO, Wednesbury —— WED 1686 Pat Boone, Shirley Jones **APRIL LOVE** (u) James Craig, **GHOST DIVER** (u)

High Street, Harborne, July 1958.

Dave Jones, in his Austin Somerset Convertible, just purchased from Potters Motors, Washwood Heath Road, Alum Rock. Stockland Green, 1958.

Singer, Shirley Bassey, listens to a music box shortly after opening the Infantile Paralysis Fellowship garden fete, Edgbaston, 5th September 1958.

Alderman Ernest Apps and Councillor Rob Pryke try out the dodgem cars at the annual Mop, Kings Norton Green, 6th October 1958.

Section Leader Coates calls the roll of Special Constables, Bordesley Green Police Station, 1958.

The Lord Mayor and Lady Mayoress, Alderman and Mrs D. Johnstone, visit Gosta Green television studios and meet the singing trio, the Beverley Sisters, 28th October 1958.

TELEVISION was blamed for a fall off in bus passengers in Birmingham.

Christmas shopping did not help the situation, either.

Alderman L. Chaffey, chairman of the Transport Committee, said: "Cinemas and theatres are still losing their fight with TV and the consequence is fewer people on the buses."

For all that, the department was making a profit in 1958 — £135,000 in the first half of the financial year with high hopes that the year carrying into 1959, would end up with a profit of £288,500.

Vespa scooter is the main prize, in a competition at the Gaumont Cinema, 12th November 1958.

Broad Street, c 1958.

The new year of 1959 came in on skates with below-freezing temperatures.

Then gale-force winds left a trail of havoc across the Midlands.

Raging blizzards sank a fishery protection vessel, Freya, and the captain went down with his ship.

Yorkshire villages were cut off by snow drifts; they were ski-ing in 18 degrees of frost at Newcastle - under - Lyme; one in ten of the phones between London and Birmingham went out of action and the A.A. described conditions as "Siberian."

Next came the smog.

For the Midland air was filthy in those days., Birmingham had only four smokeless zones.

On January 13, 1959, smog blanketted the Midlands.

Hundreds of people were taken to hospital during January and early February suffering from the effects of smog.

But what people will most remember 1959 for was the wonderful summer. It began in May and went on almost continuously into October. There were grass fires all over the Midlands and hundreds of factory workers were sent home from Cadbury's because the chocolate wouldn't set.

Conybere Street, Highgate, New Year's Day, 1959.

Rann Street/Wood Street, Ladywood, 19th January 1959.

The Royal Oak, Great Lister Street, Nechells, 1959.

Bull's Head, Hatchett Street, Hockley, 5th February 1959.

Alcester Road South, Kings Heath, c 1959.

Lonnie Donegan entertains the local branch of his fan
club, Sherlock Street, 13th February 1959. He then
appeared in a Midnight Matinee at the Alexandra
Theatre. The Skiffle King had hits with "Rock Island
Line" and "Cumberland Gap" and novelty songs such
as "My Old Man's a Dustman".

Henry Street/Heneage Street, Vauxhall, February 1959

Hit Parade singer, David Whitfield, signs photographs for
his fans, Lewis's, 6th March 1959. He went on to star in
"The Desert Song", numerous pantomimes and to adapt
his act successfully for the emerging clubland, here and in
Australia. His hits included "Cara Mia" and "Answer Me".

Broad Street, seen from Easy Row, 1959.

Woodbridge Road, Moseley, 9th March 1959. Note the "ice cold milk" dispensing machine.

The Alexandra Theatre Repertory Company, 1959.

Sausage snack
From Mrs. E. Irons, 70 Brookvale Park Road, Erdington.

IN my courting days George and I used to go to the Coliseum Picture House, Saltley.
We would buy a bag of scratchings and 1lb. of pork sausage, and find a seat in the back row of the circle.
Out would come the sausages. I would take one end and George the other and there we would sit munching away, until we had enough and then out would come the scratchings.

Film star, Yul Brynner, arrives at the Grand Hotel, Colmore Row, 20th March 1959. He was on tour promoting "Solomon and Sheba".

Watching the working models, Engineering Hall, Museum of Science and Industry, Newhall Street, 22nd March 1959.

Teenage idol, Tommy Steele, is treated for a bruised ankle, during the Television All Stars vs the Midland Old Stars football match, BSA, Small Heath, 3rd April 1959.

Digbeth, with Milk Street on the left, 1959.

Everything stops for the workforce to meet the Lord Mayor, Alderman D. Johnstone, in the trimming shop at Mulliners Ltd., (motor body builders), Bordesley Green Road, 16th April 1959.

The Lord Mayor, Alderman J.H. Lewis, preparing to open the extensions to the main runway, Elmdon Airport, 1st June 1959.

Suffolk Street, with Swallow Street on the left and the imposing building of the College of Commerce, 9th June 1959.

112

Snow Hill, from the Colmore Row/Steelhouse Lane junction, 24th June 1959.

The launch of the famous Austin Mini, Longbridge, 1959.

Birmingham Co-operative Society Ltd., Butchery
Dept. outing, c. 1959.

Elkington Street School skittle ball players, Aston, 1959.
The teacher is Miss Webster.

The interior of J. Doctor's chemist shop,
High Park Corner/Nechells Park Road,
18th August 1959. If you look at the top of page
40, in "Memories of Birmingham," you can see
the exterior of the same shop, taken on the
same day.

Eastgates Café, Slade Road, Erdington, 1959. It was very popular
with young people because it was the first in the area to have a
jukebox.

The Prime Minister, Rt Hon Harold Macmillan, acknowledges the crowds, as he leaves the Grand Hotel, September 1959.

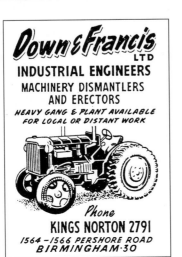

Navigation Street, looking towards Stephenson Street, 8th October 1959.

115

The Lord Mayor, Alderman J.H. Lewis, stands in front of the model Cenotaph erected in the grounds of Birmingham Cathedral, as part of the British Legion's Garden of Remembrance, 2nd November 1959.

Smallbrook Street/Horse Fair, 2nd December 1959. The film showing at the Scala was "Blind Date", starring Hardy Kruger and Stanley Baker. Seven months later the cinema closed.

Summer Row, prior to demolition, 11th December 1959.

22 RADIO EXCHANGE & SERVICE 22

GOODBYE TO AN OLD FRIEND

The last day of the Theatre Royal, New Street, 15th December 1956. It had served the city for over 183 years.

The cleaning staff have a last cuppa before cleaning up prior to the 5pm and 8pm performances.

The finale of the final show of the "Fol-de-Rols". The principal comedian is Leslie Crowther (centre), the leading lady Kathleen West (on his right) and the second comic is Charlie Stewart (with bowed head).
By the strangest coincidence, Alton, wearing the same costume and operating the same marionette as Leslie Crowther, appeared in the last show that the company ever gave in a theatre, in summer season, 19 years later, at the De La Warr Pavilion, Bexhill-on-Sea.

"Auld Lang Syne" from the audience, including the bearded Bishop of Birmingham, the Rt Rev Dr. J.L. Wilson. At the end of the show a whole procession of stars appeared on stage, demonstrating the enormous regard that the theatrical profession had for the theatre.

Back Cover: The last tram through the city centre, Steelhouse Lane, 4th July 1953.

ACKNOWLEDGEMENTS

(for providing photographs, for encouragement and numerous other favours)

Neil and Joan Allen; Norman Bailey; The Birmingham City Council Dept. of Planning and Architecture; The Birmingham Post and Mail Ltd; Nell Blackburn; Charlie Bottrill; Jim Boulton; Rose Brawn; Ron Butler; Cadbury Ltd.; Dave and Kath Carpenter; Castle Bromwich Cricket & Sports Club; David and Pauline Conway; Alan and Brenda Cronshaw; John Everett; David Goodyear; Heirlooms Collectables; George and Anne Huxley; Jo James; Paul James; Anne Jennings; Dave, Thelma and Tom Jones; Danny King; John Landon; Charles Latter; Alfred Mason; Keith Mason; Betty Milne; Dennis Moore; Dick Moore; George Peace; David Perrins; Eric Reeves; Mary Robertson; Bob Shepherd; Keith Smart; Maurice Tedd; Bert and Joyce Tredwell; Brenda Treagust; T.S. Vindicatrix Association; Terry Wallace; Joan Wanty; Bob and Joan Wilkes; Rosemary Wilkes; Alf Young.

Please forgive any possible omissions. Every effort has been made to include all organisations and individuals involved in the book.

Norman Evans, appearing as the Dame at the Theatre Royal for the pantomime season, meets the children at the annual Sparrows' party, Town Hall, 8th January 1954.